THIS CANDLEWICK BOOK BELONGS TO:

_____

_____

_____

_____

To Chris—
for the magical summer of rings and wheels and circles
J. H.

To my brother John
M. C.

Text copyright © 1994 by Judy Hindley
Illustrations copyright © 1994 by Margaret Chamberlain

First U.S. paperback edition 1996

The Library of Congress has cataloged the hardcover edition as follows:

Hindley, Judy.
The wheeling and whirling-around book / written by Judy Hindley ;
illustrated by Margaret Chamberlain.—1st U.S. ed.
(Read and Wonder) Summary: A lively celebration of circles, disks, spheres,
and all sorts of things that roll and spin.
ISBN 1-56402-490-3 (hardcover)
1. Wheels—Juvenile literature.   2. Disks, Rotating—Juvenile literature.
[1. Wheels.   2. Disks, Rotating.]   I. Chamberlain, Margaret, ill.   II. Title.   III. Series
TJ147.H56   1994
531.8'11—dc20   93-28125

ISBN 1-56402-989-1 (paperback)

2 4 6 8 10 9 7 5 3 1

Printed in Hong Kong

This book was typeset in M Bembo.
The pictures were done in ink, watercolor, gouache, and acrylic paint.

Candlewick Press
2067 Massachusetts Avenue
Cambridge, Massachusetts 02140

CANDLEWICK PRESS
CAMBRIDGE, MASSACHUSETTS

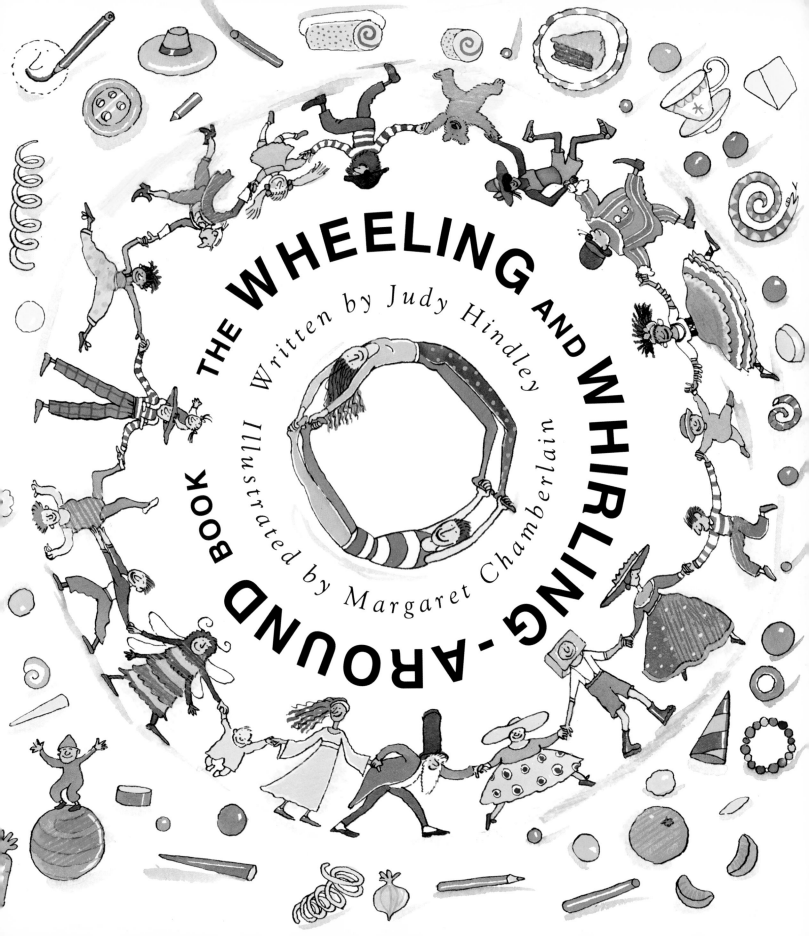

THE WHEELING AND WHIRLING-AROUND BOOK

Written by Judy Hindley

Illustrated by Margaret Chamberlain

Let us think for a bit about round things

and things that spin and whirl—

things that wheel and reel and roll

and curve and coil and curl—

things that are round

like a ball is round,

and things that are round

like a wheel,

and things that swing

in orbital rings,

out and about

and back again . . .

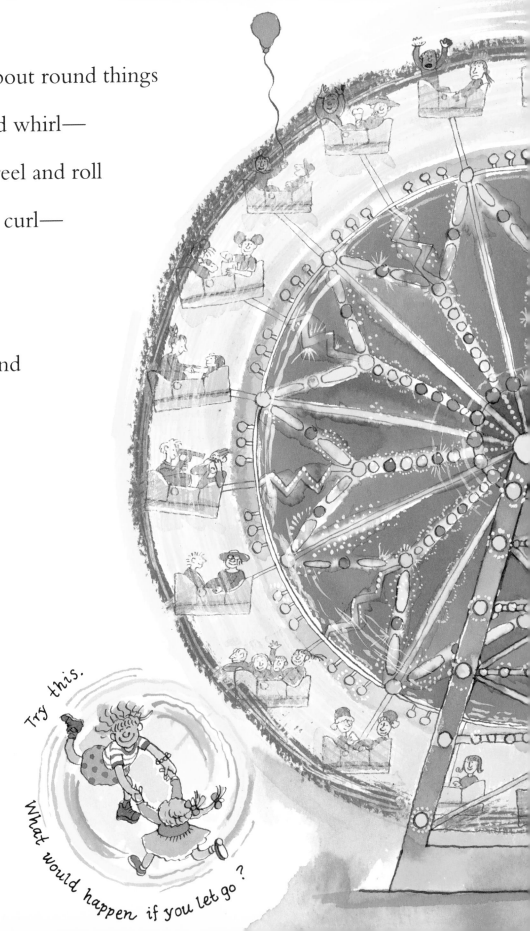

When something
spins, two opposite things
are happening at once:
flying-apartness and
holding-togetherness.

Try this.

What would happen if you let go?

An orbit is the path of something traveling around something else.

and things you can

run your fingers around,

in a spiraling slope,

like an ice-cream cone;

and things you can hug,

like a tree.

Let us muse and gaze

and ponder,

and let our thoughts go free.

Let's give our eyes a wander

and see what we can see!

cone

cylinder

flat spiral

conical spiral

Something dropped in the water makes it ripple into circles.

Every point on the rim of a circle is exactly the same distance from the center.

Try this.
Draw a circle on paper and cut it out to make a paper disk. Now keep folding it in half... then open it out.
Do you see how all the folds meet in the center?

A pizza is disk-shaped.

disk

WHERE'S MY HAT?

The imaginary line through a disk or sphere, around which it spins, is called its axis. Here's where the axis is on this disk.

A circular shape can do some things that other shapes can't do...

Let us begin

with things that spin

if you flip them along on the ground.

You can do it with coins and bottle tops;

you can do it with rings and crowns,

or dinner plates, or trash can lids,

or the rim of your grandfather's hat . . .

You can race them or chase them or bowl them away

to be driven along by a breeze,

and they sometimes whizz quite a way like that

and go speeding along with ease,

till they finally falter and wibble and wobble and drop

on the side that's flat.

ghostly circle

ghostly arc

But what if you twirl

a thinnish disk

until it's a perfect blur?

You'll find what you've made

in a ghostly way

is the every-way-round of a sphere.

ghostly sphere

ghostly ring

Round like a pea

or a Ping-Pong ball,

or the eyes at the top of your face;

like marbles and cherries

and egg yolks, and just about

everything orbiting way out in space!

Oh, a twirlable sphere is a great sort of shape,

but think what a terrible mess it can make!

Imagine a scatter of peas or pearls

or spherical sweets in a bag that has burst—

how perfectly ghastly to have in the street;

how disastrous to have on the stair!

For anything perfectly rollable

will be rolling to

everywhichwhere!

A sphere is the most common natural shape. Most huge things in the universe are spheres, like the billions of stars and planets in space.

Stars and planets are shaped into spheres by the holding-together force called gravity.

If you dumped all the water from a swimming pool in space, it would become one vast water drop. (Imagine diving in and out of it!)

Most of the tiniest natural things are spheres, like droplets and bubbles, and the eggs of zillions of small creatures.

Clinging and holding-togetherness makes droplets into spheres.

Now, unlike a ball or a globe or a sphere,

a wheel doesn't happen a lot by itself.

It has to be made by the hands or the tools

of a human, like me or like you.

And why do we bother to do such a thing?

Because of the way these remarkable shapes

will do what we want them to do.

You can yoke them on axles,

or link them on pulleys,

or fit them with spokes and dials and hubs

and pointers that spin from a circular nub,

and spools within, and sprocketed rims,

and tires, fat or thin . . .

We could muse all day upon wheels and reels

and the magical tricks of cogs!

But now let us think how a disk or a wheel

is a lot like a slice . . .

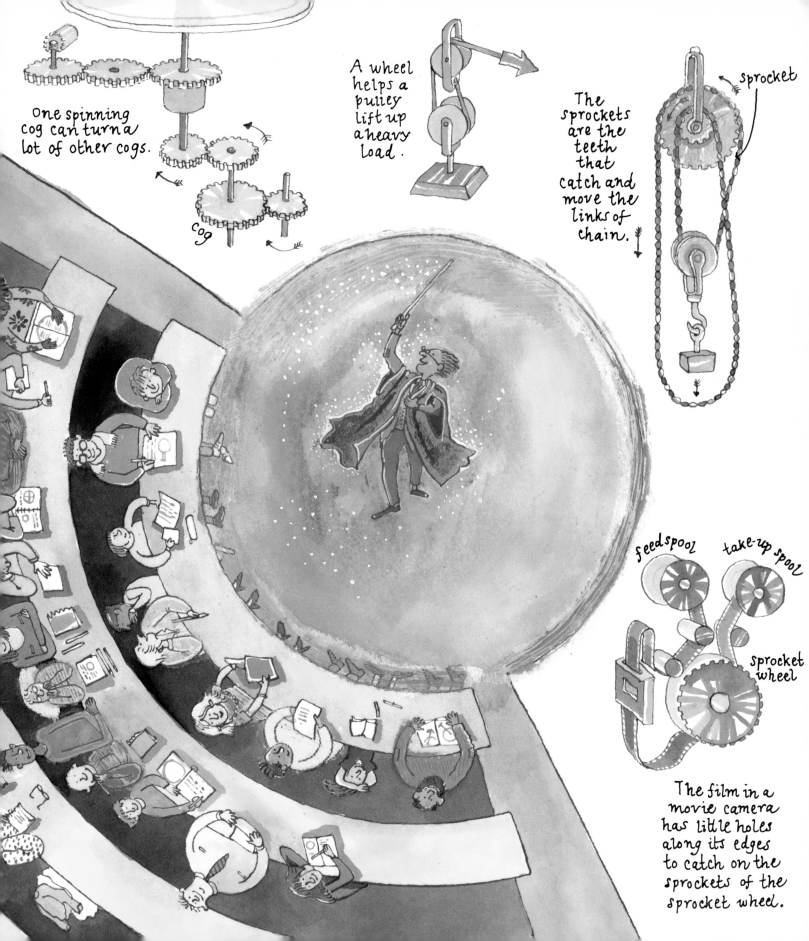

One spinning cog can turn a lot of other cogs.

cog

A wheel helps a pulley lift up a heavy load.

sprocket

The sprockets are the teeth that catch and move the links of chain.

feedspool   take-up spool

sprocket wheel

The film in a movie camera has little holes along its edges to catch on the sprockets of the sprocket wheel.

Rollers are very useful cylindrical shapes.... Logs were used to roll things, before people thought of slicing them to make wheels.

of a log—

a long

cylindrical shape.

Now perfect cylinders,

smooth and straight,

are also usually human-made.

Just think about pencils

and candles,

and your grandmother's

rolling pin;

and jars in a number of sizes

with a number of things within.

What about churns and urns, and tubs

in which the laundry spins—

Rollers are good for flattening roads.

A line of rollers can be used to make a conveyor belt.

A pair of rollers can squeeze and flatten woodpulp into paper.

What shape is a knitting needle?

and spools

and tubes and

drums and pipes

and drinking straws,

and the crown of a hat?

And what about pistons

and rollers and rods

that make an engine go?

Now . . .

you can see you can make

a cylindrical shape

out of wheel upon wheel upon wheel.

But what if you sliced the skin of it off

in a curling, coiling peel?

Instead of stacks of wheels and rings,

what you'd have is spiraling springs—

that all go around and up (or down)

like telephone cords or the springs in a bed.

Some are tight like the springs in a bike,

and some will stretch to the length of a line

and snap right back again!

But a spiraling curve can be also observed

in the coil of a snake or a butterfly's nose.

It can slope down the side

of a slide or a screw,

or circle us up in a stair—

A flat spiraling paper coil will drop into a loopy 3-D spiral if you hang it up. Try it and see!

can swoop us down, or whirl us up,

or carry us out and away—

can be flat as a spiral galaxy,

or the coil of a spider's web . . .

or go funneling in

like a whirlwind

or water that glugs

from a tub.

No wonder

we yearn

to spin and turn

and go whirling

around

in rings—

from the tiniest atom

to weather and stars,

there are so many

swirling

and orbiting

things!

Oh, let us dance

and sing, as . . .

It's not surprising we like to spin-like everything else, we're actually made of invisibly tiny spinning bits called atoms.

In addition to spiral galaxies there are spherical, egg-shaped, and even blobby ones.

If you look through a powerful telescope you can see the spiraling shapes of distant galaxies like ours.

All the planets, moons, and stars in the galaxy are spheres .... The spinning Earth and its moon orbit the sun .... Our sun is a star in the arm of a spiraling galaxy like a great expanding pinwheel.... Even the sun is spinning.

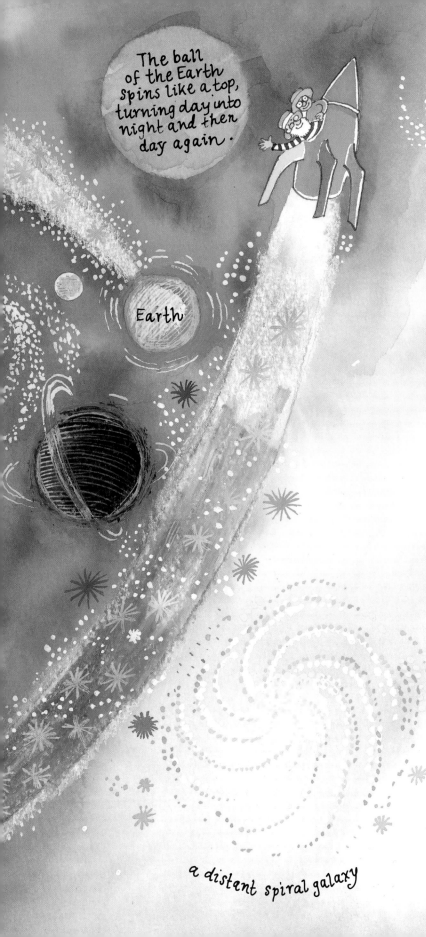

The ball of the Earth spins like a top, turning day into night and then day again.

Earth

a distant spiral galaxy

we all go around

the day again,

and we all go around the sun,

and we all go around the galaxy

in the curl of its glittering arm!

See how the giddiest games

we play,

and the tiniest things there are,

echo out

through the traveling universe,

unraveling star by star—

and it's all a part

of the dance of things,

the spinning-aroundness

and spiraling rings,

however small, however near,

however vast and far.

How many
round and circular
and spinning things
can you find
in this book?

JUDY HINDLEY, a graduate of the University of Chicago, worked in children's book publishing for many years before turning to writing full-time. About *The Wheeling and Whirling-Around Book,* she says, "It was a completely wacky book to do. I had planned a book about wheels and cogs. But roundness is so mystical, and everything goes around, so it became a book about much more." Judy Hindley has written more than thirty books for children, including *A Piece of String Is a Wonderful Thing, Into the Jungle,* and *The Big Red Bus.*

MARGARET CHAMBERLAIN has illustrated more than fifty books for children, including Judy Hindley's *A Piece of String Is a Wonderful Thing.* She says she particularly enjoyed working on *The Wheeling and Whirling-Around Book* because "everything you can think of in life is round. There were so many things I could put into the pictures."